CONTENTS

HOW TO USE THIS GUIDE

This London volume of the *City Cycling* series is designed to give you the confidence to explore the city by bike at your own pace. On the front flaps is a locator map of the whole city to help you orient yourself. Here, you will see five neighbourhoods to explore: Soho and Mayfair (p. 10); Shoreditch (p. 16); Borough (p. 22); Notting Hill (p. 28); and Hampstead (p. 34). All are easily accessible by bike, and are full of cafés, bars, galleries, museums, shops and parks. Each area is mapped in detail, and our recommendations for places of interest and where to fuel up on coffee and cake, as well as where to find a Wi-Fi connection, are marked. Take a pootle round on your bike and see what suits you.

For maps of the whole city, turn to the back. These detailed maps show bike routes, and roads to avoid, across a large section of central London. They'll help you navigate safely, and pinpoint everything you need, from bike shops to 'Boris bike' docking stations, landmarks and more. If you fancy a set itinerary, turn to A Day On The Bike on the front flaps. It takes you on a relaxed 25km (16-mile) route through some of the parts of London we haven't featured in the neighbourhood sections, and visits some of the more touristy sights. Pick and choose the bits you fancy, go from back to front, and use the route as it suits you.

A section on Racing and Training (p. 40) fills you in on some of London's cycling heritage and provides ideas for longer rides if you want to explore the beautiful countryside around the city, while Essential Bike Info (p. 44) discusses road etiquette and the ins and outs of using the cycle-hire scheme and public transportation. Finally, Links and Addresses (p. 48) will give you the practical details you need to know.

LONDON: THE CYCLING CITY

London: a busy, confusing city, both sprawling and congested at the same time? Or one of the greenest cities in the world, where you can ride for miles through parks and along canals without seeing a car; a succession of characterful villages that are easily navigable – and best discovered – by bike? Truth is, both descriptions are true on their day; but the UK capital has a rapidly developing and increasingly inclusive bike culture. It is the home of the original Tweed Run, a leisurely, celebratory ride for the sartorially inclined, and an important outpost of the global Bicycle Film Festival phenomenon. For years cycling was seen as a minority interest, with 1980s commuters describing themselves as the 'lunatic fringe'. Bicycles now throng London's streets but, sadly, many attribute the boom in part to the bombings in July 2005, which drove many workers away from public transport; once they got on their bikes, some never took the Tube again.

Today London is a cycling city. Check out Clerkenwell Road, the so-called 'Hipster Spice Route', during rush hour for proof of the bicycle boom. Twice a day this main east–west artery is jammed full of cyclists commuting from the eastern boroughs into the centre of town, and back again. Elsewhere, the King's Road and the Embankment bring bankers in from the southwest; Kennington Road, workers from the south; and the mainline stations daily disgorge thousands of suits from the leafy Home Counties, who unfold their Bromptons and pedal to work. But London's bicycles are not just commuters' tools. More than in any other European city, you'll see all of cycling's tribes out to play: skinny-jeaned kids on track bikes, Pashley princesses, bearded guys on tourers and roadies. A big part of the resurgence is down to Londoners embracing cycle sport – both participating and watching. The recent top performances at London 2012 of Chris Hoy and Victoria Pendleton on the track and Bradley Wiggins in the time trial, as well as Wiggins and Mark Cavendish in the Tour de France, have helped turn London cycle mad. In 2014, the Tour de France will visit London for the second time in seven years, which is sure to see spectators packing the streets.

At the weekends, Regent's Park in central London and Richmond Park far to the west can seem like hamster wheels for the city's road cyclists, but London can also be seen at a much more leisurely pace – and the leisure cyclist's secret weapon is the so-called 'Boris bike'. The nickname comes from London's floppy-fringed, bike-riding mayor Boris Johnson, who oversaw the introduction of the Barclays Cycle Hire scheme (to give it its proper name) in 2010 – though it was his predecessor, Ken Livingstone, who approved the project. Johnson has said that he hopes the bikes will become as common in the capital as black cabs and red buses, and they are slowly taking over the streets, making a huge difference to Londoners' lives. The roads are noticeably more cycle-friendly these days, so get on a Boris bike and, heavy and uncool though it is, even a short cycle – past Sadler's Wells theatre, say, or along the Mall – is great fun.

Details on how to use the docking stations can be found in Essential Bike Info (p. 44), so there's no excuse not to get one. Take it for a spin across Waterloo Bridge, and see Tower Bridge, the City and St Paul's to the east; to the west, the Houses of Parliament, Battersea Power Station and that famous Waterloo sunset. You can't go fast, you look a bit ridiculous, and so you smile.

NEIGHBOURHOODS

SOHO & MAYFAIR

FOR HIGH FASHION, CONTEMPORARY ART
AND ROCK 'N' ROLL

Soho and Mayfair sit side by side, just a hop from one to the other across the grand terraces of Regent Street. They are hemmed in to the north by the dangerous, congested Oxford Street, with Piccadilly and Leicester Square forming the southern boundaries. To the west is Park Lane (again, a cycling no-go); east are the bustling shopping streets and piazza of Covent Garden. They are two neighbourhoods – one well-to-do, one slightly down-at-heel – which make for an interesting day's exploring away from the glitzier tourist sights of central London.

Soho was green fields until the 1660s (around the time of the Great Fire of London in 1666), and its development never took off in the grand style of Marylebone or Mayfair, its neighbours to the north and west. By the nineteenth century, it had been taken over by music halls, theatres and seedy nightlife, and to an extent that hasn't changed. Mayfair, on the other hand, was developed mainly by the Dukes of Westminster, the Grosvesnors, after whom one of the most imposing squares was named. These days Mayfair is home to embassies, luxurious hotels and some of the most expensive apartments in

the world. Yet, though genteel, all bowler hats and hedge funds, it's also quietly dedicated to the pursuit of pleasure – nightlife, fine restaurants and couture, all coloured by at least a whiff of the dissolute.

Start in the southwest, perhaps at **Shepherd Market** ①, a beautifully tranquil square. Near here, both Keith Moon of The Who and Mama Cass of the Mamas and Papa died, four years apart, in the same flat on <u>Curzon Street</u>, and in <u>Half Moon Street</u> both Boswell and Bertie Wooster were residents – albeit fictionally, in the case of the latter – at different times. Another odd Mayfair pair are George Frideric Handel and Jimi Hendrix, who lived in adjoining flats in <u>Brook Street</u> – Handel for over thirty-five years from 1723 until his death in 1759, and Hendrix for two in the 1960s, in what he called his 'first real home'. The now-interconnected property forms the **Handel House Museum** ②, which cleared rooms in 2011 for an exhibition commemorating the fortieth anniversary of Hendrix's death.

On the way there don't miss the elegant <u>Mount Street</u>, full of cigar shops, fashion boutiques and fine dining, or the lovely **Mount Street Gardens** ③, tucked away between the Victorian mansion blocks. Elsewhere in Mayfair is **Stella McCartney** ④ on <u>Bruton Street</u>, various gentlemen's outfitters on <u>Savile Row</u> and <u>Jermyn Street</u>, and more contemporary threads at **Dover Street Market** ⑤. <u>Cork Street</u> and its environs are home to a host of private galleries and art dealers, specializing in the best contemporary art and interior design. Alongside the Royal Academy, **Burlington Arcade** ⑥ has traditionally been home to upmarket jewellers, many of whom still trade there, while **Gray's Antiques Market** ⑦, around the corner from Claridge's hotel, is a rabbit warren of antiques stalls, a nice counterpoint to the area's chi-chi boutiques. Other cultural hotspots include the **National Gallery** ⑧ and the **Photographers' Gallery** ⑨, which has a good bookshop.

Just off Regent Street, the dividing line between Soho and Mayfair, is **Liberty** ⑩, the famous department store in its mock-Tudor building; nearby is **Rapha Cycle Club** ⑪, the road-cycling brand's flagship store, which has beautiful memorabilia, good coffee, cakes and Wi-Fi. For something more substantial (unless, of course, you have a wallet bulging enough for **Scott's** ⑫, a seafood restaurant

and Mayfair institution), pedal over into Soho for cheaper food and drink. There's every sort of cuisine imaginable – from BBQ to Indian street food, bratwurst to sushi, mainly to service the appetites of the advertising and media types who work there. New lunch places pop up by the hour, and the restaurant sensation du jour changes almost as often. Frith Street, Poland Street and D'Arblay Street are good bets. While in the area, check out **Phonica** ⑬ and **Black Market Records** ⑭, both respected shops representing two different generations of London's dance-music history. Or, for a different sort of dance, there's the equally legendary **Ronnie Scott's Jazz Club** ⑮.

Carnaby Street, despite its history, is not worth visiting. Try Newburgh Street instead, or duck into **Kingly Court** ⑯ for more boutiques, or back rubs and yoga if it all gets too much. **Flat White** ⑰, **Nordic Bakery** ⑱ and **Fernandez & Wells** ⑲ serve good coffee, but none beats **Bar Italia** ⑳ for ambiance. This is where an older generation of cyclists went for updates on the Giro d'Italia, when continental cycling was a world away and the only source of information was the pink *Gazzetta dello Sport*. By night, Soho can be loud and sleazy... and fun. Start the night at **The John Snow** ㉑, a pub named after the doctor who deduced that the source of London's cholera epidemic was a local water pump. There are a few remaining sex shops in Walker's Court, but the rest of Soho is brash entertainment. Old Compton Street, meanwhile, is one of the central points of London's gay nightlife.

REFUELLING

FOOD	DRINK
Bodean's ㉒ for American-style ribs	**The Blue Posts** ㉔ and **Pillars of**
Ray's Jazz ㉓, the café in a record shop (in a bookstore), for sandwiches and coffee	**Hercules** ㉕ are legendary pubs in Mayfair and Soho, respectively

WI-FI
Brunch and browse at **The Breakfast Club** ㉖

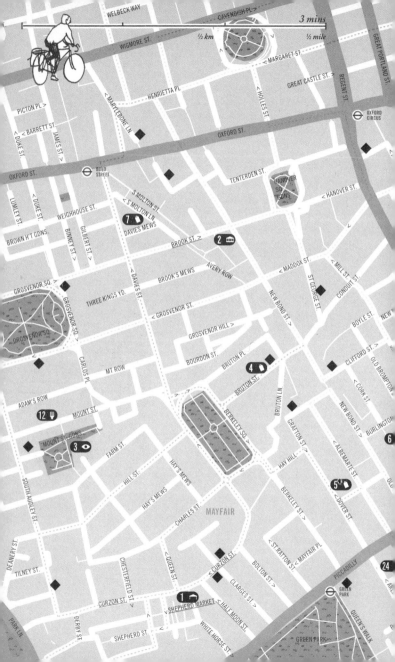

SHOREDITCH

Jump back twenty years or so and this part of East London was very different: empty warehouses, raves, YBAs and, in <u>Brick Lane</u>, textile industries and a large Bangladeshi community. The artists have moved on (head to Hackney Wick, off-map, for something more cutting edge), but the area remains vibrant. It is also undoubtedly the capital's city-cycling heartland.

To the south lies the City, London's financial heart, well worth a cycle at the weekends when the streets are deserted; to the north, the grand housing of De Beauvoir Town and lots of quiet routes up to Dalston (see main map, a destination for good Turkish food and hip nightlife). Between here and the West End is Clerkenwell, London's design and architecture quarter, and **Smithfield** ①, which hosts a meat market by day (the area has been associated with livestock for over a thousand years) and great restaurants and bars by night.

If you're coming from the west, be sure to stop at bike café **Look Mum, No Hands** ② (see also A Day On The Bike). It has a good workshop, great food and regular exhibitions of bikes and bike-related art. West to east there are quiet

back roads to take, as well as the canal, but Old Street is a main commuter route, and is busy but manageable. **<u>Whitecross Street</u>** ③ is also good for food, from the varied market stalls at lunchtime or in restaurants at night (it's best to avoid the pubs and restaurants on Old Street itself). Dive down Leonard Street to **The Book Club** ④, a bar and venue for cultural events; alternatively, there are bars, cafés and bookshops on <u>Rivington Street</u>. Across Shoreditch High Street, <u>Redchurch Street</u> is also good for galleries and bars, and is where **Labour and Wait** ⑤ can be found for beautiful, old-fashioned homewares, along with **Albion** ⑥, a bakery and café that also does brunch

– or pick up some fresh fruit and cheese for a picnic in nearby **Arnold Circus** ⑦. **Hoxton Square** ⑧ was home to the original White Cube gallery and seminal club Blue Note; now there are yet more bars, and, on sunny days, a fashion parade ranging from the sublime to the ridiculous. Head up Hoxton Street for a quiet pint at **The Red Lion** ⑨, or further up to **The Macbeth** ⑩ for grungier entertainment.

Some of London's most famous markets are in the area: **Columbia Road** ⑪ for plants and flowers (Sundays), and **Spitalfields** ⑫ for food and more touristy fare. Brick Lane also has a street market on Sundays, selling bric-à-brac, clothes, second-hand goods and nonsense, though some of the most interesting things – salvage, antiques and vintage fashion – can be found just off it, in the yard behind **Truman Brewery** ⑬ and along Cheshire Street. Careful on your bike, as it gets very crowded! Brick Lane is also a nightlife destination, and is crammed with bars and venues. Eat at any one of the numerous curry houses (they'll vie for your business, and it's impossible to pick a favourite). For something a bit more authentic from the Indian subcontinent, try the Original Lahore Kebab House or Tayyabs, both further south in Whitechapel (off-map).

Across the road from the easterly end of Columbia Road is **Hackney City Farm** ⑭. Visit the pigs and then go into the café for

great bacon – the best fried breakfast in East London! There's a bike workshop there, too. Finally, pedal up Goldsmith's Row to **Lock 7 Cycle Café** ⑮ at the bottom of Broadway Market (off-map), and then cycle back into town along Regent's Canal, stopping in at **Towpath** ⑯, a charming café just below Whitmore Bridge.

REFUELLING

FOOD	DRINK
Rochelle Canteen ⑰ for exquisite food served in an old school bike shed	**Nude Espresso** ⑱ for the best antipodean coffee, or **Pretorius** ⑲, for coffee and cake in a nice road-bike workshop

WI-FI
Fix Coffee ⑳ and **The Old Shoreditch Station** ㉑
both have free wireless

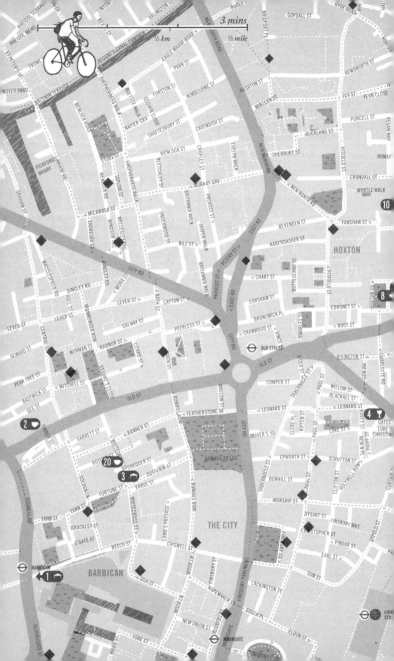

BOROUGH

A FOODIE PARADISE, WITH QUIRKY MUSEUMS
AND THE RIVERBANK

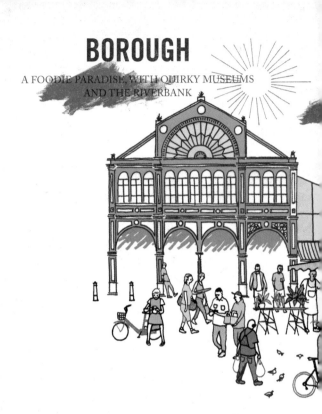

Cycle south over the river – taking **Tower Bridge** ①, perhaps, passing the **Tower of London** ②, and you'll be cycling a bit slower on the way back, such are the foodie delights of Bermondsey and Borough, two adjacent neighbourhoods on the river in Southwark. We're pedalling the area bounded by Tower Bridge Road to the east, Blackfriars Road to the west and Long Lane to the south – though clubbers among you may want to head further south to the **Ministry of Sound** ③, the original London super-club. Cycling home is not recommended!

First, let's head a little further east of Tower Bridge, to the beautiful nineteenth-century shipping warehouses of <u>Butler's Wharf</u> and Shad Thames, where the **Design Museum** ④ sits fronting the river (until 2014, that is, when it will relocate to Kensington). It would be

wrong to call the area south of here 'gritty', but there are boarded-up buildings, salvage yards (full of interesting furniture and fittings) and, nestled among them under the railway arches, **Maltby Street Market** ⑤ (Saturdays), which has quietly become a local foodie hotspot, threatening to overshadow its more famous rival, <u>Borough Market</u>. One of the capital's best coffee purveyors, **Monmouth Coffee Company** ⑥, has an outpost here, and is open to the public on market days, when it's flanked by stalls selling cheeses, fish, tapas and cured meats. From here, it's only a short hop to **Bermondsey Square** ⑦, which is also taken over by farmers' market stalls on Saturdays; on Fridays it hosts one of London's best antiques markets.

Bermondsey Street, meanwhile, is much more upmarket, a far cry from the tanneries that once lined it. Today you'll find independent boutiques, hip restaurants, as well as cafés and two well-established gastropubs, **The Woolpack** ⑧ and **The Garrison** ⑨, opposite each other. There's even London's only **glassblowing studio** ⑩. Reflecting the history of the area is the **Fashion & Textile Museum** ⑪, while the newest branch of the **White Cube** ⑫, the largest of the gallery's sites, is a new arrival. Other quirky museums in the area include the **Old Operating Theatre** ⑬ for a glimpse into Victorian surgical conditions and techniques, and the **Kirkaldy Testing Museum** ⑭, which showcases some gigantic Victorian engineering technology. And, of course, on the river, there is the behemoth that is the **Tate Modern** ⑮, a somewhat shopping mall-esque museum in a former power station, with an impressive collection of modern art starring all the greatest masters of the twentieth century and beyond.

The riverside path is worth a slow pedal, though the crowds and some narrow sections mean you won't get much faster than that, and may have to walk. Heading east from the Tate, you'll pass **Shakespeare's Globe** ⑯, the **Clink Prison Museum** ⑰ (a notorious gaol that gave rise to the phrase 'in the clink' in the seventeenth century), and a replica of Sir Frances Drake's *Golden Hinde*. Beyond London Bridge is **City Hall** ⑱ – though Southwark Bridge is also worth a look. It's perhaps the prettiest of the Thames bridges, and has a rare example of a segregated bicycle superhighway – take it north towards St Paul's Cathedral (off-map).

Don't leave the area without locking your bike to a lamp-post and nosing around **Borough Market** ⑲ (full market Thursday–Saturday, lunch only Monday–Wednesday) for fresh farm produce, fish and game, fine chocolates, cheeses, and almost anything else you might want to eat – it's London's premier foodie destination. As far as restaurants go, **Elliot's Café** ⑳ serves new British cuisine using only ingredients from the market. For something more old school, try **Maria's Market Café** ㉑, an institution where the hostess has been serving bubble and squeak since the 1960s. Or, for a drink away from the hubbub, **The George Inn** ㉒ is London's only surviving galleried coaching inn (Borough High Street used to be lined with them). Shakespeare, Pepys and Dickens were all regulars in their time.

One final place to note: **The Shard** ㉓, Renzo Piano's mixed-use building, the tallest in Europe, which now dominates the newly minted London Bridge Quarter. If you have a minute, and deep pockets, take one of the lifts up to the public galleries on floors 68–72, for unmatched views of London.

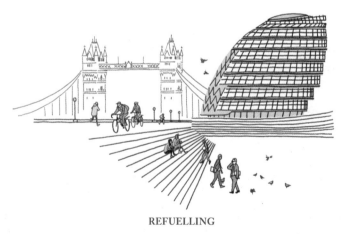

REFUELLING

FOOD	DRINK
Del'Aziz ㉔ is a great Middle Eastern deli, and the **Tate Modern café** ⑮ is busy but pleasant	**Total Organics Juice Bar** ㉕ will do you a revitalizing juice when Borough Market's open

WI-FI
Bermondsey Street Coffee will get you online ㉖

NOTTING HILL

VINTAGE HEAVEN, PORTOBELLO MARKET
AND GOOD EATING

For some, Notting Hill is synonymous with Prime Minister David Cameron and his chums, celebrity chefs and Hugh Grant; for others, the neighbourhood is all about the Notting Hill Carnival (the biggest street party after Rio de Janeiro, but in August), <u>Portobello Road</u> and its market (half junk, half antique gems), and the eclectic boozers, record shops and vintage boutiques that surround it. It's this mix of cultures, high life and street life, that makes the area so interesting.

The streets of Maida Vale, north of Warwick Avenue (off-map), are pleasant to cycle through, but we'll be concentrating on the area bounded by the Grand Union Canal at its northern edge, Bayswater Road to the south, Ladbroke Grove out west and Queensway in the east. Mostly these streets are wide, leafy and quiet, flanked by huge, white terraced houses – either split into flats, or grandly occupied by a single owner, complete with keys to the private gardens in the square outside. Only a few, including **Pembridge Square** ①, **Colville Square** ②, and **Kildare Gardens** ③, are open to the public. Bayswater Road, though busy, is wide, and isn't too bad to cycle along.

The best way to approach Notting Hill is either through Hyde Park and up through the back streets, or along the narrow

boat-strewn canal, past Little Venice, perhaps taking a moment to stop in at the **Waterside Café** ④ or **Puppet Theatre Barge** ⑤, or to watch the skaters in **Meanwhile Gardens** ⑥. Then cycle over the humpbacked bridge and into Golborne Road, where the smell of baking at **Lisboa Patisserie** ⑦ hits you (they do deliciously authentic Portuguese tarts) and you dodge people carrying antiques and furniture. Further down, by **Pizza East** ⑧ (lock your bike outside and sit on the street) there are tasty whiffs of Moroccan tagine, Trinidadian curry or fried fish, depending on which of the canvas stalls in **Golborne Road Market** ⑨ are serving up. Don't leave this north end of Portobello without gawping at **Trellick Tower** ⑩, Ernő Goldfinger's brutally impressive tower block, or stopping for a coffee at **Lowry & Baker** ⑪. Also tucked away is **Slack Cycling** ⑫, a super-exclusive cycling boutique where they'll measure you up for a bespoke frame, or a jersey. Apart from Fridays, it's appointment only. Further south, there's the nice, independent **Bicycle Workshop** ⑬.

Portobello Road Market ⑭ itself can be a bit of a scrum – especially at the weekends – so it's best to dismount and walk down. In any case, you won't want to travel fast: there's so much to see,

and the characters selling the antiques, furniture, clothes and general tat are almost as fascinating as their goods. If it all gets too much, **The Tabernacle** ⑮, an art gallery, café and community centre, has a bike-friendly sun-trap terrace for relaxing on. Or if you want to take more in, there are cookware, interiors, design and fashion boutiques on and around <u>Westbourne Park Road</u> and, on <u>Blenheim Crescent</u>, **The Travel Bookshop** ⑯, made famous by the film *Notting Hill*. For foodies, there's **Books for Cooks** ⑰, and **The Spice Shop** ⑱ for inspiration and exotic ingredients. Notting Hill is also famous for its record shops: recommended are the eclectic and respected **Honest Jon's Records** ⑲ and **Rough Trade** ⑳.

Head west of Ladbroke Grove to explore the grand crescents; the quieter roads east of Portobello are home to swish restaurants, including the Michelin-starred **Ledbury** ㉑, and the quirky **Museum of Brands, Packaging and Advertising** ㉒. Other good eating options include **Osteria Basilico** ㉓, and **Fez Mangal** ㉔ and **Durbar Tandoori** ㉕, which do quality Turkish and Indian food, respectively. Wend your way back into town through the posh promenading and shopping spot that is <u>Westbourne Grove</u>, or cross Bayswater Road and cycle down <u>Kensington Palace Gardens</u>. It's virtually traffic-free and the houses and embassies are fantastic; one sold in 2004 to Lakshmi Mittal, the steel baron, for £57 million. Watch out for ambassadors and oligarchs!

REFUELLING

FOOD
The two Notting Hill branches of Arancina ㉖ ㉗ are good for an Italian carb fix

DRINK
Raoul's Café ㉘ will quench your thirst and also does a great eggs Benedict

WI-FI
Coffee Plant ㉙ on Portobello Road is good for lattes, leaf teas and free surfing

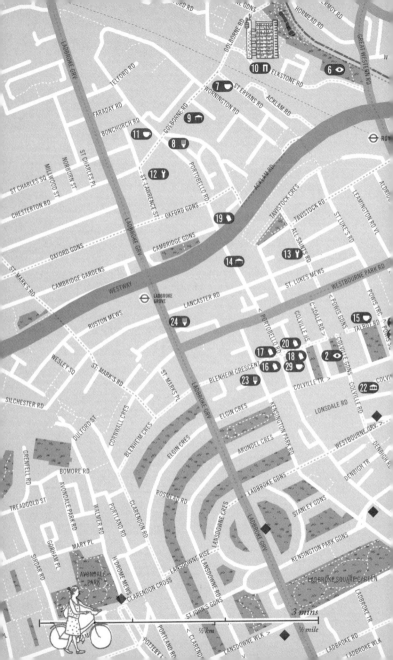

HAMPSTEAD

GREEN SPACES, GRAND ARCHITECTURE
AND FAMOUS RESIDENTS

Come to Hampstead, a genteel, leafy neighbourhood with strong literary, artistic and musical associations, and you'll encounter something in short supply on the rest of your London travels: hills. The most direct route there is up Haverstock Hill, a long drag from Camden, but if you're feeling lazy it's easy to take the train to **Hampstead Heath station** ① instead. It's a good place to start your visit to the famous heath, a vast slice of near-wilderness not too far from the centre of town. London Overground trains usually accept bicycles outside rush hour, but it's best to check first (see Links and Addresses for National Rail details).

If you are brave enough to cycle, take a breather halfway up, turning right off the main road, just before Belsize Park tube station, to see the **Isokon Building** ② on Lawn Road, a Modernist masterpiece designed by Wells Coates. Former residents include Bauhaus luminaries Walter Gropius and László Moholy-Nagy, as well as artists Henry Moore, Barbara Hepworth and Ben Nicholson … and Agatha Christie, too. It's tempting to imagine the conversations that must have gone on late into the night in the in-house drinking den,

the Isobar. From here, it's more pleasant cycling up to Hampstead proper through the back streets. The quickest route to the heath is to head up Parliament Hill, past **George Orwell's house** ③, on which is the first of many plaques commemorating famous local residents; over the years William Hogarth, William Blake, Alfred Tennyson, Anna Pavlova and Kingsley Amis have all called Hampstead home.

Dismount to climb the final part of **Kite Hill** ④, where on windy days you'll see kites flying with the whole of London behind them – from the Arsenal football stadium to Anish Kapoor's 'helter-skelter' sculpture (more properly known as the Orbit) in the Olympic Park, to St Paul's Cathedral (now dwarfed by The Shard; p. 25), Canary Wharf and the London Eye. Many of the paths on the heath are pedestrian-only, but it's great to explore by bike, and searching out the cycle routes is worth it for the parade of local dogs being walked. If you're hot, take a dip in the bathing ponds, either the **mixed ponds** ⑤ or the **men's** ⑥ **and women's** ⑦, also called Highgate Ponds, which, for the adventurous and foolhardy, are open daily, year round.

Leaving the Heath by the ponds, you're at the bottom of Hampstead village, and bang in the middle of some impressive architecture. <u>Keats Grove</u> is a good example; the poet John Keats lived in the street from 1812 to 1820. His house, where he fell in love with Fanny Brawne and wrote some of his most famous poems, including 'Ode to a Nightingale', is now the **Keats Museum** ⑧ (Sigmund Freud's old place has been similarly revamped as the **Freud Museum** ⑨, which holds fascinating exhibitions connecting art and literature with psychoanalysis). <u>Downshire Hill</u> is very grand, while **Two Willow Road** ⑩ is a Modernist masterpiece, built by Ernö Goldfinger as his family home. Today the house is owned by the National Trust, but at the time it was built not everyone was impressed. Local resident Ian Fleming even campaigned against its construction – some say this is the source of his mega-villain Auric Goldfinger's surname!

Take it slowly while cycling up through the picturesque back streets of Hampstead Village, perhaps stopping for a drink or some food at chi-chi gastropub **The Wells** ⑪, or, further up, **The Flask** ⑫. There are also numerous independent cafés clustered off the High Street; try **Simply Scrumptious** ⑬ for food, **Mani's** ⑭ for cake. Then up around <u>Frognal Rise</u>, admiring the beautiful houses and the numerous plaques dotted around – **John Constable's** ⑮ on Lower Terrace (you can also visit the artist's grave at **St John-at-Hampstead** ⑯), or the architect Sir George Gilbert Scott's at Admiral House – up, up, up to Whitestone Pond. Out of breath yet? Relax: this is the

highest point in London, and the site of the **Hampstead Observatory** ⑰ at the top of the hill. From here, head past (or into) **The Spaniards Inn** ⑱, a purported haunt of Dick Turpin, but definitely take a detour to **Kenwood House** ⑲. This Robert Adam-designed building was given to the nation in 1927; it holds an art collection with works by Vermeer, Rembrandt, Constable, Turner and Gainsborough, and the manicured lawns are host to outdoor concerts in summer.

Highgate, further on, is perhaps best known for its **cemetery** ⑳ on Swain's Lane, a lung-busting cycling hill climb. People as diverse as Karl Marx, Douglas Adams and Christina Rosetti have their final resting place here (some of the cemetery is only open to official tours). But it is also a quaint village, filled with welcoming pubs: **The Wrestlers** ㉑ has a cosy fire in the winter and a brilliant atmosphere; and Highgate's own **Flask pub** ㉒ is particularly cycle-friendly.

REFUELLING

FOOD	DRINK
The Red Lion & Sun ㉓ is a gastropub in Highgate with seriously good food	Oliver's Village Café ㉔ in Belsize Village is a nice pit stop for tea and cake

WI-FI
Ginger & White ㉕ serves great coffee and has free Wi-Fi

19 🏛

21 ⚓

23 ⚲

HAMPSTEAD LN

HIGHGATE HIGH ST

CHOLMELEY CRESCENT

ARCHWAY R

3 mins

½ km

½ mile

22 ⚲

SOUTH

HIGHGATE HILL

FITZROY PK

WATE

7 👁

HOLLY LODGE GDNS

HILL WAY

20 👁
HIGHGATE
CEMETERY

MERTON LN

HIGHGATE
CEMETERY

HIGHGATE WEST HILL

MAKEPEACE AVENUE

SWAIN'S LN >

MILLFIELD LN

6 👁

CHESTER RD

SWAIN'S LN

Hampstead Heath

4 👁

CROFTDOWN RD

YORK RD

DARTMOUTH PARK RD

DARTMOUTH PARK HILL

3 👁

BOSCASTLE RD

CHETWYND RD

SPENCER RISE

PARLIAMENT HILL

TANZA RD

TWISDEN RD

INGESTRE RD

NASSINGTON RD

HIGHGATE RD

SAVERNAKE RD

GOSPEL
OAK

GORDON HOUSE RD

MPSTEAD
ATH

NTINE RD

AGINCOURT RD

RHINEHART RD

SHIRLOCK RD

RODERICK RD

COURTHOPE RD

ESTELLE RD

RONA RD

DAM VILLAGE

FORTESS RD

FLEET RD

MANSFIELD RD

SOUTHAMPTON RD

VICAR'S RD

GRAFTON RD

2 👁

GARNETT ST

UPPER PARK RD

PARK HILL RD

LAWN RD

VICAR'S RD

WEEDINGTON RD

GRAFTON RD

FALKLAN

KENTISH TOWN

REGIS RD

ISLIP ST

SIZE

OWNSIDE DR

MALDEN RD

QUAD' GRV

QUEEN'S CRESCENT

SPRING PL

HOLMES ST

GRAFTON TERRACE

BASSETT ST

MALDEN R

HOLMES ST

RACING AND TRAINING

When London hosted the Tour de France in 2007 – only the third time the race had come to the UK – nobody quite knew what to expect: would the Brits take to the Tour? They needn't have worried. The prologue and the subsequent stage to Canterbury were attended by millions of cycling fans, confirming that professional cycling was now big news.

London 2012 saw Britain's track cyclists again dominate the sport, this time on the home turf of the **London Velopark**, one of the venues for the Olympic Games in East London, which will open to the public in 2014. Bradley Wiggins won the **men's individual time-trial event** in Surrey (see Links and Addresses for a map of the course) – along with a certain small stage race in France – and the resultant surge in cycling participation means that the city's cycle clubs are booming, its high-end bike shops numerous, and its popular training roads chock-a-block with cyclists on weekday evenings and weekends. In fact, the Olympic Games had visited London twice before: in 1908, bicycle polo featured as an exhibition sport; and, tucked away in a corner of southwest London, the **Herne Hill Velodrome** (off-map) is the only surviving venue from the 'austerity' games of 1948. Recently resurfaced, this outdoor concrete-banked track holds national-level track events, and until recently hosted the Good Friday meeting, which attracted some of Europe's top talent. Still in regular use by local clubs, the facilities are run by **Velo Club Londres**, which organizes open training sessions, and a track league.

When it comes to road riding, such is the size and complexity of London that riders tend to stick to their areas – heading out north if they live in North London, east if they live in Hackney and its environs, and so on. The Surrey and Kent hills, to the southwest and southeast, respectively, are probably the classic training territory for London's cyclists; many of the city's historic cycling clubs are based in the southern suburbs. Box Hill, near Dorking, Surrey, is famous for its zig-zag road, which, though only 2.5km (1.5 miles) long and with an average gradient of 5 per cent, is the closest you'll get to an Alpine climb in these parts. For the Kent hills, many cyclists and clubs meet at **Café St Germain** in Crystal Palace (off-map), for a quick espresso before rolling out. Alternatively, if you'd like to join an

organized, friendly road ride, there's one departing from the **Rapha Cycle Club** (p. 12) a couple of times a week. On Saturday mornings, the ride alternates between heading east to Essex and south to Surrey; on Thursday nights it heads for nearby Regent's Park for a few quick laps – check the website (see Links and Addresses) for details and up-to-date information.

If you're looking for a quick, simple training spin, Regent's Park, in central London, or Richmond Park to the southwest (off-map) are both regular spots for the capital's cyclists. Regent's Park is a flat, 4km (2.5 mile) loop with light traffic. Every weekday evening, as long as the weather's good, you'll find cyclists there; in the summer, on Tuesdays and Thursdays in particular, the park becomes crammed with speeding bikes. As long as you don't mind taking your turn on the front, people are usually very friendly, and don't object to people joining their train. Richmond Park, not being so central, is more of an easy weekend destination for most. The outer perimeter road loops 11km (7 miles) and takes in a couple of small climbs. It's a picturesque place and, with the large herds of deer, it's easy to forget that you're close to the centre of a major city! Again, the park's riders are generally friendly.

For targeted hill training, Londoners often head to the northern suburbs of Highgate and Hampstead (see pp. 34–39 for a neighbourhood guide). These offer a range of short, sharp climbs to test your legs on. The classic is Swain's Lane in Highgate, which cuts through the famous cemetery (p. 37). A fearsome and gloomy 800m (half-mile) stretch, which ramps to around 20 per cent near the end, it's the site of London club **Rollapaluza**'s Urban Hill Climb competition, which takes place in July. For links for racing and training routes, please see Links and Addresses.

Finally, if you need any good road kit – from tyres to jerseys, or a whole new bike – a good place to start is **Condor Cycles**, a London-based frame-builder who has kept premises on Gray's Inn Road since 1948, and is the best independent shop in the city. Its workshop is usually very busy, so if you need any urgent bike repairs, also try **Bespoke Cycling**, in Farringdon Road, or **Pretorius** (p. 19), near Old Street. **Kinoko Cycles**, meanwhile, is a specialist road shop from urban brand Tokyo Fixed, and is located in the heart of Soho.

ESSENTIAL BIKE INFO

London's cyclists are a hardy lot, but cycling around the capital doesn't have to be an ordeal. The roads are getting friendlier, and by picking and choosing where you go, you will stay safe and have a good time.

ETIQUETTE

As in all big cities, cyclists in London come in all forms, from the slow, safe and law abiding to the kamikaze. Some tips for the visitor are:

- Do not assume cars have seen you, or will give way. Unlike some European cities, London's drivers do not necessarily put cyclists first.
- Bus lanes are OK to ride in, and can be something of a sanctuary, but keep an eye out for motorbikes and scooters, which are also allowed in.
- Do not jump red lights, even though some others do – it's likely they know the junction well.
- Do not pass other cyclists on the left. Go around them as you would if overtaking in a car.
- Do not ride on the pavement.

SAFETY

London's roads can be narrow in comparison with other European capitals, and for many visitors cycling on the left is a new experience. Unfortunately, accidents are all too common in the capital, and the mayor has been criticized for putting cyclists' lives at risk by not prioritizing their safety more highly. The **Barclays Cycle Superhighways** initiative, for example, is widely thought to be a waste of money. Although the cycle paths are well signposted along key commuting routes, their critics say they are little more than blue paint on the road, frequently interrupted by bus stops, parked cars and junctions. Even when on a designated cycle lane, keep your eyes and ears open to what's going on around you. Some other tips are:

- Place yourself out of the gutter, and more than 1m (about 3 ft) away from parked cars.
- Advanced stop lines are rarely respected; it's OK if you feel vulnerable to manoeuvre yourself out ahead of the traffic in front of the lights.
- Watch out for lorries. There have been too many injuries in the

past few years caused by cyclists caught in the blind spot, often when the HGV is turning left. Do not pass lorries on the inside, and remember that if you can't see the mirrors, the driver can't see you – even if he or she is looking. It's better to wait behind them than get caught out.

SECURITY

London's bike thieves are highly sophisticated and acquisitive! Always secure your bike when you leave it: lock it to something solid. If leaving it at night, or in a quiet part of town, make double-sure you're happy with the lamp-post or stand. Look at the other bikes locked around that area as a guide to what locals feel is safe, and always err on the side of caution.

FINDING YOUR WAY

If you were hoping for an easy-to-follow, rational system of bike routes in the capital, prepare for disappointment. There aren't that many dedicated cycle paths, and you'll save yourself hassle if you understand that the blue cycle-route signs will probably let you down. They do mark sensible, bike-friendly and often picturesque routes, but they have a tendency to appear and disappear, leaving you in the lurch. You'll probably see a lot of Londoners on them, but it's likely they'll have memorized the route as part of their commute. Our advice is stick to map reading.

Help is at hand, in the form of the **Legible London** panels. They're springing up all around town, with maps and useful information for walkers and cyclists. They are on the Barclays Cycle Hire docking stations (see below), and you'll even find them on the canals. Since there's no grid system to London's roads, do not try and take shortcuts, thinking that the road will logically snake back through.

CITY HIRE BIKES

The **Barclays Cycle Hire** scheme is easy to use and, while no longer as cheap as it was, the bomb-proof bikes, though a bit heavy and unwieldy, are fun. Initially available only in the centre of town, in 2012 the scheme was expanded east towards the Olympic Park and west to Shepherd's Bush, meaning that it covers almost the entire area mapped in this guide. It's also now increasingly available in south and southwest London.

Every 300m (984 ft) to 500m (1,640 ft) around town, you'll see bikes lined up in docking stations. Tourist offices and some tube stations have leaflets explaining the scheme, and there are apps available pinpointing the nearest docking station, and how many bikes are available. London residents or frequent visitors can pay for membership and annual access (currently £90), but tourists and casual users just need to turn up at their closest docking station (marked with a ◆ on the city maps) with their credit cards at the ready. It costs £2 a day, or £10 for a week.

To hire a bike, use the touchscreen terminal at the end of the dock. The process is quite long, but the instructions are easy to follow. If you want a bike there and then, the machine will eventually print you out a code; tap the code into an occupied dock and, when the green light shows, pull the bike out. Once you're rolling, you have 30 minutes of free riding. If you don't dock the bike within that time, you pay £1 for an hour and £4 for 90 minutes, with the bike getting ever more expensive as time goes on. It's designed to encourage you to dock the bikes quickly, so if you're going on a long journey, think about making a stop along the way (you'll have to wait five minutes before you take another bike). If you arrive at your destination and the docking station is full, press a button on the screen for an extra 15 minutes free riding, then check the map for the closest station.

When you leave the bike, push it firmly back in, until you see the green light. If the bike is broken, press the red 'fault' button on the dock. Unlike in Paris, there are no locks on the bikes, so it's best to use them for short trips, and pick up a new one when you need it.

OTHER PUBLIC TRANSPORT

London Underground and the city's buses do not accept non-folded bicycles, but you can take a bike on the river bus service run by **Transport for London**. **Thames Clippers**, which runs the Tate-to-Tate boat between Tate Britain and Tate Modern (p. 24), also accept bikes, although bike parking on them is limited.

The companies that operate London's many overground rail services all have different bicycle policies; it's best to check the **National Rail** website for details. As a rule, however, expect that it will be difficult or impossible to take a non-folding bike on a train during rush hours (approximately 7–10am and 4–7pm).

TRAVELLING TO LONDON WITH BIKES

Eurostar is the best way to travel to London with your bike from European destinations. There are direct services to London from Paris, Brussels and Lille, and Avignon and Aix-en-Provence during the summer months. There are also simple connecting services from Amsterdam, Cologne, Geneva and Lyon. Between London, Paris and Brussels you can – for a fee – reserve a bike space on the train. This means you can simply arrive at the station and take the bike to a goods carriage, where it is hung up for the journey. Make sure you reserve in advance and arrive in plenty of time, since the freight depots are a long way from the passenger terminal. As of 2013, all bikes in bags longer than 85cm (33 in.) – i.e., all non-folding bikes – must be sent via the registered baggage service. The 'Turn Up and Go' option, where you leave your bike bag at a counter in the check-in hall, costs £10 each way. Folding bikes can be taken on as carry-on luggage, but they too must be in a bag smaller than 85cm in length.

If you're arriving at any of London's airports, it's best to keep your bicycle in its case for the journey in to town. Only **London City Airport** in East London is OK to ride to and from; **Heathrow** is technically possible, but you'll be riding on some busy A-roads. The others are just too far out. All UK train services will accept a bicycle in a box, and it is possible to take a bike box on the Tube. Unless your journey is pretty direct, rush-hour travel with bulky luggage on the Underground is not advised, as the trains get very full.

HIRING BIKES

Thanks to the size of the city, it's possible to find a great range of bikes available for hire. Hire shops, however, are thin on the ground. All in all, we'd recommend using the Barclays Cycle Hire scheme bikes, but if you'd like to hire from somewhere else – or if you want to go outside the Barclays zone, or want a road bike – then we recommend **Cloud 9 Cycles** for Dutchies, **Velorution** for Bromptons, **Foffa** for single-speeds and **On Your Bike** for hybrids and road bikes (see Links and Addresses for details).

LINKS AND ADDRESSES

Albion
2–4 Boundary Street, E2 7DD
albioncaff.co.uk

Arancina
• 19 Pembridge Road,
  W11 3HG
• 19 Westbourne Grove,
  W2 4UH
arancina.co.uk

Barbican Centre
Silk Street, EC2Y 8DS
barbican.org.uk

Bar Italia
22 Frith Street, W1D 4RP
baritaliasoho.co.uk

Bermondsey Square
bermondseysquare.co.uk

Bermondsey Street Coffee
163–167 Bermondsey Street,
SE1 3UW
streetcoffee.co.uk

Black Market Records
25 D'Arblay Street, W1F 8EJ
bm-soho.com

Bodean's
10 Poland Street, W1F 8PZ
bodeansbbq.com

Books for Cooks
4 Blenheim Crescent, W11 1NN
booksforcooks.com

Borough Market
8 Southwark Street, SE1 1TL
boroughmarket.org.uk

British Library
96 Euston Road, NW1 2DB
bl.uk

Bunhill Fields
38 City Road, EC1Y 1AU
cityoflondon.gov.uk

Burlington Arcade
51 Piccadilly, W1J 0QJ
burlington-arcade.co.uk

Café St Germain
16–17 Crystal Palace Parade,
SE19 1UA
cafestgermain.com

Camley Street Natural Park
12 Camley Street, N1C 4PW
wildlondon.org.uk

City Hall
The Queen's Walk, SE1 2AA
london.gov.uk/city-hall

Clink Prison Museum
1 Clink Street, SE1 9DG
clink.co.uk

Coffee Plant
180 Portobello Road, W11 2EB
coffee.uk.com

Columbia Road Market
Columbia Road, E2 7RG
columbiaroad.info

Del'Aziz
5 Canvey Street, SE1 9AN
delaziz.co.uk

Design Museum
28 Shad Thames, SE1 2YD
designmuseum.org

Dover Street Market
17–18 Dover Street, W1S 4LT
doverstreetmarket.com

Durbar Tandoori Restaurant
24 Hereford Road, W2 4AA
durbartandoori.co.uk

Elliot's Café
12 Stoney Street, SE1 9AD
elliotscafe.com

Exmouth Market
Exmouth Market, EC1R 4QL
exmouth-market.com

Fashion & Textile Museum
83 Bermondsey Street, SE1 3XF
ftmlondon.org

Fernandez & Wells
43 Lexington Street, W1F 9AL
fernandezandwells.com

Fez Mangal
104 Ladbroke Grove, W11 1PY
fezmangal.com

Fix Coffee
161 Whitecross Street,
EC1Y 8JL
fix-coffee.co.uk

Flat White
17 Berwick Street, W1F 0PT
flatwhitecafe.com

Freud Museum
20 Maresfield Gardens,
NW3 5SX
freud.org.uk

Ginger & White
4a–5a Perrin's Court, NW3 1QS
gingerandwhite.com

Gray's Antiques Market
7 Davies Mews, W1K 5AB
graysantiques.com

Green Park
royalparks.org.uk

Hackney City Farm
1a Goldsmith's Row, E2 8QA
hackneycityfarm.co.uk

Hampstead Heath station
South End Road, NW3 2QD
nationalrail.co.uk

Hampstead Observatory
Lower Terrace, NW3
hampsteadscience.ac.uk

Handel House Museum
25 Brook Street, W1K 4HB
handelhouse.org

Hardy Tree
St Pancras Old Church,
Pancras Road, NW1 1UL

Highgate Cemetery
Swain's Lane, N6 6PJ
highgate-cemetery.org

Honest Jon's Records
278 Portobello Road, W10 5TE
honestjons.com

Houses of Parliament
St Margaret Street, SW1A 0AA
parliament.uk/visiting

Keats Museum
10 Keats Grove, NW3 2RR
keatshouse.cityoflondon.gov.uk

Kenwood House
Hampstead Lane, NW3 7JR
english-heritage.org.uk

Kingly Court
Kingly Court, W1B 5PW
carnaby.co.uk

Kirkaldy Testing Museum
99 Southwark Street, SE1 0JF
testingmuseum.org.uk

Labour and Wait
85 Redchurch Street, E2 7DJ
labourandwait.co.uk

Liberty
Regent Street, W1B 5AH
liberty.co.uk

Lisboa Patisserie
57 Golborne Road, W10 5NR

London Glassblowing Studio & Gallery
62–66 Bermondsey Street, SE1 3UD
londonglassblowing.co.uk

Lowry & Baker
339 Portobello Road, W10 5SA
lowryandbaker.com

Maltby Street Market
Maltby Street, SE1 3PD
maltbystmarket.com

Mani's
12 Perrin's Court, NW3 1QS

Maria's Market Café
Borough Market, SE1 1TL
boroughmarket.org.uk

Meanwhile Gardens
Elkstone Road, W10 5NT
meanwhile-gardens.org.uk

Ministry of Sound
103 Gaunt Street, SE1 6DP
ministryofsound.com

Monmouth Coffee Company
34–36 Maltby Street, SE1 3PA
monmouthcoffee.co.uk

Museum of Brands, Packaging and Advertising
2 Colville Mews, W11 2AR
museumofbrands.com

National Gallery
Trafalgar Square, WC2N 5DN
nationalgallery.org.uk

Natural History Museum
Cromwell Road, SW7 5BD
nhm.ac.uk

Nordic Bakery
14A Golden Square, W1F 9JG
nordicbakery.com

Nude Espresso
26 Hanbury Street, E1 6QR
nudeespresso.com

Old Operating Theatre Museum
9a St Thomas Street, SE1 9RY
thegarret.org.uk

Oliver's Village Café
92 Belsize Lane, NW3 5BE
oliversvillagecafe.com

Osteria Basilico
29 Kensington Park Road, W11 2EU
osteriabasilico.co.uk

Phonica
51 Poland Street, W1F 7LZ
phonicarecords.com

Photographers' Gallery
16–18 Ramillies Street, W1F 7LW
thephotographersgallery.org.uk

Pillars of Hercules
7 Greek Street, W1D 4DF

Pizza East
310 Portobello Road, W10 5TA
pizzaeastportobello.com

Portobello Road Market
portobellomarket.org

Puppet Theatre Barge
Little Venice, W9 2PF
puppetbarge.com

Raoul's Café
105–107 Talbot Road, W11 2AT
raoulsgourmet.com

Ray's Jazz at Foyle's
196 Tottenham Court Road, W1T 7LQ
foyles.co.uk/rays-jazz-music

Regent's Park
royalparks.org.uk

Rochelle Canteen
Arnold Circus, E2 7ES
arnoldandhenderson.com

Ronnie Scott's Jazz Club
47 Frith Street, W1D 4HT
ronniescotts.co.uk

Rough Trade
130 Talbot Road, W11 1JA
roughtrade.com

Royal Albert Hall
Kensington Gore, SW7 2AP
royalalberthall.com

St John-at-Hampstead
Church Row, NW3 6UU
hampsteadparishchurch.org.uk

Science Museum
Exhibition Road, SW7 2DD
sciencemuseum.org.uk

Scott's
20 Mount Street, W1K 2HE
scotts-restaurant.com

Serpentine Gallery
Kensington Gardens, W2 3XA
serpentinegallery.org

Serpentine Lido
Hyde Park, W2 2UH
serpentinelido.com

Shakespeare's Globe
21 New Globe Walk, SE1 9DT
shakespearesglobe.com

Shepherd Market
Shepherd Street, W1J 7PH
shepherdmarket.co.uk

Simply Scrumptious
9 Flask Walk, NW3 1HJ
simplyscrumptiousbars.co.uk

Smithfield Market
201–232 Charterhouse Street, EC1M 6JN
smithfieldmarket.com

South Bank
Belvedere Road, SE1 8XX
southbankcentre.co.uk

Spitalfields Market
Brushfield Street, E1 6AA
spitalfields.co.uk

Stables Yard
Chalk Farm Road, NW1 8AH
camdenlock.net

Stella McCartney
30 Bruton Street, W1J 6QR
stellamccartney.com

Tate Modern
Bankside, SE1 9TG
tate.org.uk

The Blue Posts
6 Bennet Street, SW1A 1RP
taylor-walker.co.uk

The Book Club
100–106 Leonard Street, EC2A 4RH
wearetbc.com

The Breakfast Club
33 D'Arblay Street, W1F 8EU
thebreakfastclubcafes.com

The Flask (Hampstead)
14 Flask Walk, NW3 1HE
theflaskhampstead.co.uk

The Flask (Highgate)
77 Highgate West Hill, N6 6BU
theflaskhighgate.com

The Garrison
99 Bermondsey Street,
SE1 3XB
thegarrison.co.uk

The George Inn
75–77 Borough High Street,
SE1 1NH
nationaltrust.org.uk

The John Snow
39 Broadwick Street, W1F 9QJ

The Ledbury
127 Ledbury Road, W11 2AQ
theledbury.com

The Macbeth
70 Hoxton Street, N1 6LP
themacbeth.co.uk

The Old Shoreditch Station
1 Kingsland Road, E2 8AA
jaguarshoes.com

The Red Lion
41 Hoxton Street, N1 6NH
redlionhoxtonst.com

The Red Lion & Sun
25 North Road, N6 4BE
theredlionandsun.com

The Shard
32 London Bridge Street,
SE1 9SY
the-shard.com

The Spaniards Inn
Spaniard's Road, NW3 7JJ
thespaniardshampstead.co.uk

The Spice Shop
1 Blenheim Crescent, W11 2EE
thespiceshop.co.uk

The Tabernacle
34–35 Powis Square, W11 2AY
tabernaclew11.com

The Travel Bookshop
13 Blenheim Crescent,
W11 2EE
thetravelbookshop.co.uk

The Wells
30 Well Walk, NW3 1BX
thewellshampstead.co.uk

The Woolpack
98 Bermondsey Street,
SE1 3UB
woolpackbar.com

The Wrestlers
98 North Rd, N6 4AA
thewrestlershighgate.com

Total Organics Juice Bar
Borough Market, SE1 1TL
boroughmarket.org.uk

Tower Bridge
Tower Bridge Road, SE1 2UP
towerbridge.org.uk

Tower of London
Tower Hill, EC3N 4AB
hrp.org.uk

Towpath
Regent's Canal, N1 5SB
towpathcafe.wordpress.com

Trellick Tower
7 Golborne Road, W10 5NY

Truman Brewery
91 Brick Lane, E1 6QL
trumanbrewery.com

Two Willow Road
2 Willow Road, NW3 1TH
nationaltrust.org.uk

Victoria & Albert Museum
Cromwell Road, SW7 2RL
vam.ac.uk

Waterside Café
Warwick Crescent, W2 6NE

Wellington Arch
Hyde Park Corner, W1J 7JZ
english-heritage.org.uk

White Cube
144–152 Bermondsey Street,
SE1 3TQ
whitecube.com

BIKE SHOPS, CLUBS, RACES AND VENUES

For links to our racing and
training routes, please visit
citycyclingguides.com

Barclays Cycle Hire
tfl.gov.uk/roadusers/cycling

Barclays Cycle Superhighways
tfl.gov.uk/roadusers/cycling

Bespoke Cycling
143–145 Farringdon Road,
EC1R 3AB
bespokecycling.com

Bicycle Workshop
27 All Saints Road, W11 1HE
bicycleworkshop.co.uk

Cloud 9 Cycles
38 Store Street, WC1E 7DB
cloud9cycles.com

Condor Cycles
49–53 Grays Inn Road,
WC1X 8PP
condorcycles.com

Foffa
Unit 9, Pinchin Street, E1 1SA
foffabikes.com

Herne Hill Velodrome
104 Burbage Road, SE24 9HE
hernehillvelodrome.com

Kinoko Cycles
10 Golden Square, W1F 9JA
tokyofixed.co.uk

Lock 7 Cycle Café
129 Pritchard's Road, E2 9AP
lock-7.com

London Velopark
Olympic Park, E20 3EL
london2012.com/venue/
velodrome

Look Mum, No Hands
49 Old Street, EC1V 9HX
lookmumnohands.com

Men's Individual Time Trial
Surrey (44km [27 miles])
london2012.com/cycling-
road/event/men-time-trial/
coursemap

On Your Bike
52–54 Tooley Street, SE1 2SZ
onyourbike.com

Pretorius
2 Drysdale Street, N1 6NA
pretoriusbikes.com

Rapha Cycle Club
85 Brewer Street, W1F 9ZN
rapha.cc

Rollapaluza
rollapaluza.com

Slack Cycling
32B St Lawrence Terrace,
W10 5SX
slackcycling.com

Velo Club Londres
vcl.org.uk

Velorution
88 Great Portland Street,
W1W 7NS
velorution.com

OTHER USEFUL SITES

Eurostar
St Pancras International,
Euston Road, N1C 4QL
eurostar.com

Heathrow Airport
Croydon Road, TW6 1AP
heathrowairport.com

Legible London
tfl.gov.uk/microsites/legible-london

London City Airport
Royal Docks, E16 2PX
londoncityairport.com

London Underground
tfl.gov.uk/tube

National Rail
nationalrail.co.uk

Thames Clippers
thamesclippers.com

Transport for London
tfl.gov.uk

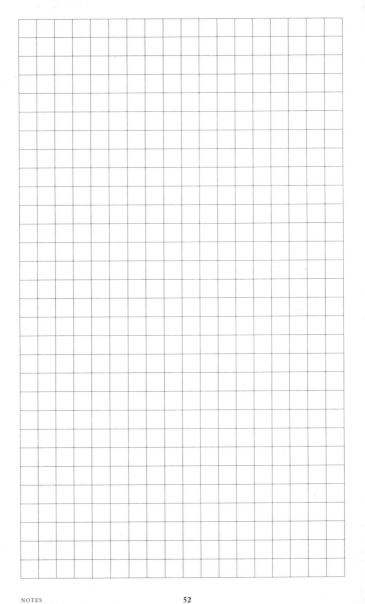

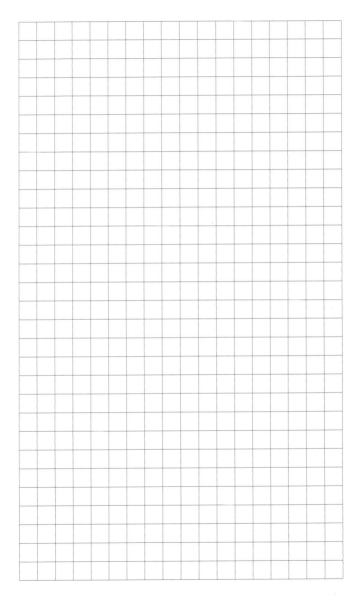

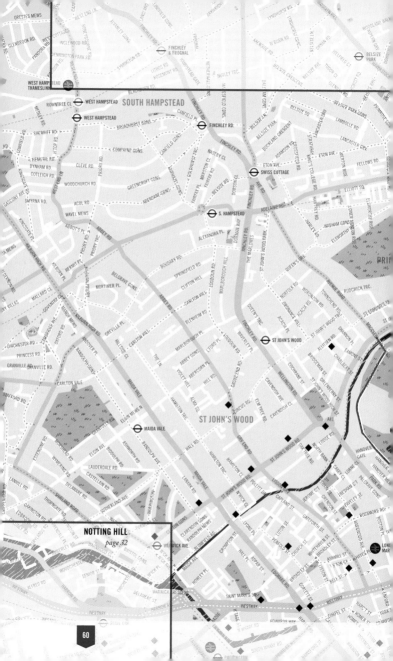

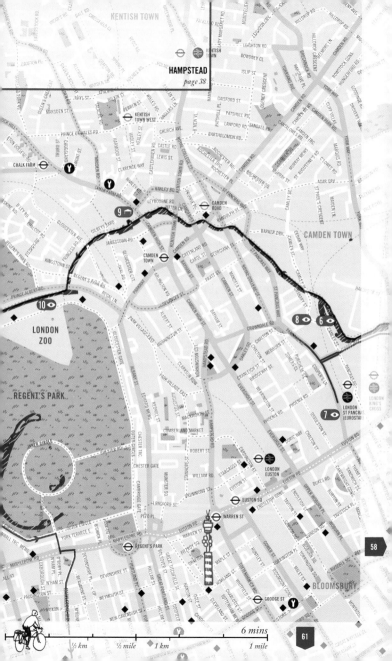

HAMPSTEAD
page 38

KENTISH TOWN

HAMPSTEAD

CAMDEN TOWN

CAMDEN TOWN

LONDON ZOO

REGENT'S PARK

LONDON ST PANCRAS (EUROSTAR)

LONDON KING'S CROSS

LONDON EUSTON

BLOOMSBURY

6 mins

½ km   ½ mile   1 km   1 mile

58

61

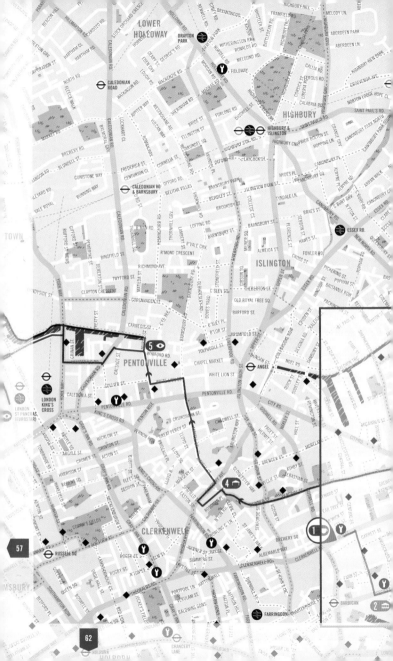

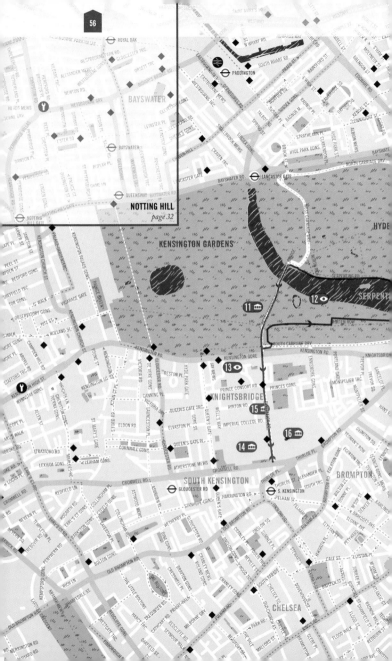

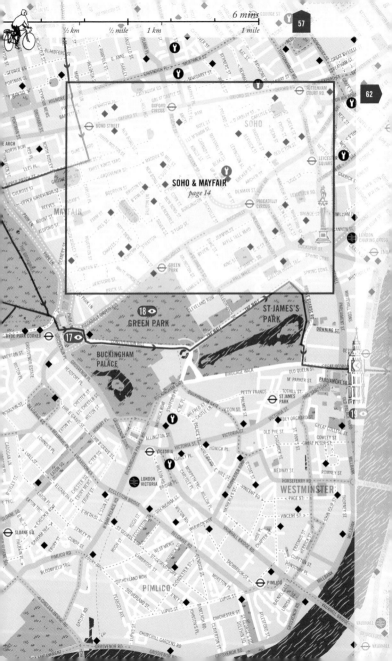

½ km   ½ mile   1 km   1 mile

SOHO

SOHO & MAYFAIR
page 14

MAYFAIR

GREEN PARK

ST JAMES'S PARK

18
GREEN PARK

HYDE PARK CORNER   17

BUCKINGHAM PALACE

DOWNING ST.

ST JAMES PARK

LONDON VICTORIA

VICTORIA

WESTMINSTER
PAGE 26

PIMLICO

PIMLICO

Rapha, established in London, has always been a champion of city cycling – from testing our first prototype jackets on the backs of bike couriers, to a whole range of products designed specifically for the demands of daily life on the bike. As well as an online emporium of products, films, photography and stories, Rapha has a growing network of Cycle Clubs, locations around the globe where cyclists can enjoy live racing, food, drink and products. Rapha is also the official clothing supplier of Team Sky, the world's leading cycling team.

Rapha.